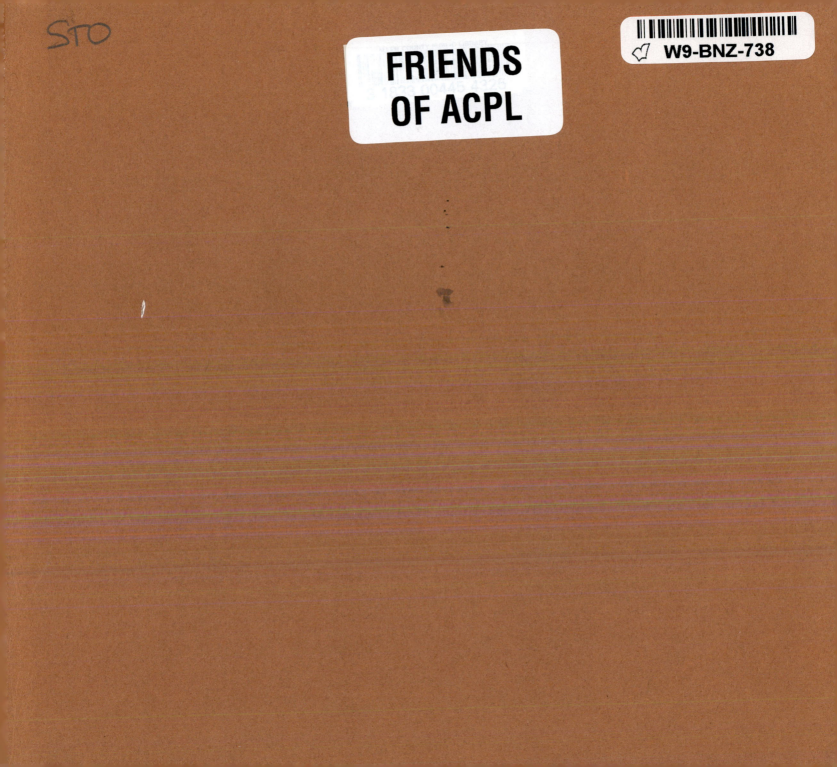

The Lifting Stone

The Lifting Stone

by ANNE ELIOT CROMPTON

illustrated by MARCIA SEWALL

Holiday House · New York

Library of Congress Cataloging in Publication Data
Crompton, Anne Eliot.
The lifting stone.
SUMMARY: Only the man who can move the huge stone
in the field shall have Wealthy's hand in marriage.
Her sister knows the secret of lifting the stone.
[1. Folklore—United States] I. Sewall, Marcia.
II. Title.
PZ8.1.C882Li   [398.2] [E]   77-10607
ISBN 0-8234-0325-4

"Mandy Jane," I told myself, "you are not pretty. In fact, you are plain." I was looking at my homely face in the kitchen dresser mirror. I stuck out my tongue, and looked downright ugly. "I don't care," I said. But I did care.

Every time I looked at my older sister Wealthy, I felt plain. Wealthy was pretty. Besides that, Wealthy was capable. She washed and wove, cooked and cleaned, baked and brewed for Papa and the boys and me. All day, Wealthy worked in the house. But sometimes she would stop work and look out at the hills, and sigh.

When Wealthy sighed, I felt bad. I knew why she sighed. She wished to marry. She particularly wished to marry Moses Fiske, who was young and fun and good looking. And I could have helped her marry.

If I had told Wealthy my secret, she could have married Moses right away. But I did not wish her to leave home. If she did, guess who would have to bake and brew, clean and cook, wash and weave? And I did not even know how to do these things. I could hay and harness, milk and mow. My best friend was Senator, our plough horse. Surely, I had no wish at all for Wealthy to marry and leave home! But I did not fret. I felt sure Wealthy would be with us forever, because of the stone.

The stone sat in our north field. It was huge and vast and enormous. It was right in the way when we went to plough. The boys swore at the stone. Years ago, Papa tried to move it out of the field. He tried with horses and oxen, with lever and fulcrum. But the stone stood.

Papa cussed out the stone for a long while. Then he walked all around it, looking at the soil and the lay of the land. He limped up to the stone wall and looked over at the spring that bubbled on the other side.

All at once, Papa turned and came back to the stone. "Don't anybody lift that stone," he told the boys. "That stone sits where she is."

"Yes, Papa," said the boys. "Of course, Papa."

When Wealthy put her hair up, neighbor men came to see her. Some of them mumbled about marriage. Then Papa made his great and famous declaration. The man who lifted the stone out of the field could marry Wealthy.

First, Ephraim Hatch tried to lift the stone. Ephraim was old and bald. But he was strong, and so was his horse. Wealthy fretted, watching him work at the stone. She twisted her apron in her hands and chewed her hair. She did not wish for Ephraim to lift that stone!

Neither did I. But I did not fret. There was only one way to lift that stone, and that was my secret. Ephraim did not know it. Ephraim and his big horse worked till sundown, then they gave up. And the stone stood.

Then Fat Bushrod tried to lift the stone. How Wealthy did fret! I wished I could tell her there was no danger, because only I knew how to lift the stone. Bushrod finally gave up, and the stone stood.

The next day, Preservèd Fish came with two oxen. Preservèd never smiled. Either he worked, or he read sermons. That was all he did. Wealthy bit her hair and twisted her apron, but in the end she smiled, for the stone stood.

Then, this spring, Moses Fiske came to try. I liked Moses, so I helped him harness up. In fact, I harnessed the horse for him, because he kept stopping work to look at Wealthy. Wealthy looked back at him and sighed.

Moses and the horse went to work. Moses gasped and strained at the lever. Sweat darkened the horse. But the stone stood.

Later, I smelled new gingerbread, so I beat a path to the kitchen. There sat Wealthy at her churn, dripping bitter tears into the butter.

I asked, "What is the matter?"

"Moses Fiske," she sobbed. "I did so wish for him to lift the stone!" She hid her face in her apron and wept.

What could I say? If I told her my secret, I would soon be left to bake and brew and so forth.

I cut a piece of gingerbread for Wealthy and left it by the churn. I cut two more, for Senator and me. Then I found my fishing pole and slipped out the door.

Up in the north field, I called to Senator. He raised his big head and perked his ears. I called "gingerbread!" Then he came galloping.

I climbed on his back. I whispered "gingerbread" in his ear. Then, goodness! How Senator did gallop! Only I knew how fast Senator could gallop, because I gave him gingerbread.

We came to the lifting stone and the stone wall. I slid down off Senator and gave him his treat. He drooled and slobbered and muttered, as if to say "thank you."

I climbed the stile into the wood lot. I came to the bubbling spring, and I followed it down to the first hidden pool. And there, for heaven's sake, I met Moses Fiske!

Moses was pretending to fish. In fact, he was just staring sadly into the water. He looked so sad I tried to cheer him up. "Tell you a secret," I said. I had a little secret Moses might like to know.

"Thank you, Mandy Jane. Never mind."

I grabbed Moses' hand anyway and pulled him to his feet. He was so weak with sadness, he let me lead him down to the next hidden pool, where the fish are. That was my little secret.

When Moses saw trout in the pool, he almost smiled. He said, "Mandy Jane, you are clever!" Now, that softened my heart. I know I am clever, but Moses was the first other person to notice it. When he caught his fifth trout Moses said, "There's few so clever as you, Mandy Jane!"

Pride puffed me up like a crowing cockerel. I said, "Tell you just how clever I am. I know how to lift the lifting stone." Moses shook his head at that, so I proved it. I told him how.

Moses dropped his fishing pole.

Then I saw what I had done. I had gone and told my big secret. I nearly wept.

Moses asked, "What is the matter?"

I sniffed and swallowed. "Now I will have to bake and brew and—"

"No," said Moses. "Wealthy will still keep house. I will move in with you."

Then I dried my tears fast! And we laid our plans. As I left I reminded Moses, "Wait for a heavy rain."

"You just have Senator's gingerbread ready," he called after me.

Next time I woke in the night and heard rain heavy on the roof, I nudged Wealthy awake. "Listen to that rain!" I said. "Go on, get up and bake." Wealthy knew our plan, so she got right up and baked gingerbread by candlelight.

In the bright early morning, Moses came to our door. He said to Papa, "Come watch me lift your stone." We all trooped out to the north field, and Ephraim Hatch, Fat Bushrod and Preservèd Fish came too.

Moses had dug a deep trench from the spring down to the lifting stone, as I had told him. Spring water and rain water rushed together around the stone, loosening the earth. I harnessed Senator and climbed on his back. I whispered "gingerbread" in his ear. Then, goodness! How Senator pulled! Only I knew how hard Senator could pull, because I gave him gingerbread.

Moses gasped and strained at the lever. Sweat darkened Senator. Water gurgled and sucked, earth sank away.

The stone was bigger than any of us had thought. As the earth washed away, more and more stone appeared. Moses groaned, and I could feel Senator giving up.

I shouted fiercely, "Ginger-bread!" Senator pricked his ears and gathered himself for one last pull.

I saw Moses look at Wealthy. One glance was all he needed. Once more he leaned on the lever, once more Senator pulled. And with a great gasp and gulp of earth and water, the stone rose.

Moses and Wealthy rushed together and hugged.

I got down and hugged Senator. Then I gave him a whole gingerbread loaf.

Ephraim Hatch and Fat Bushrod and Preservèd Fish cheered.

"Well!" said Papa, clapping Moses hard on the back. "You figured it! I was just waitin' for one of you fellows to figure it!"

Moses gurgled, "Aaaah?"

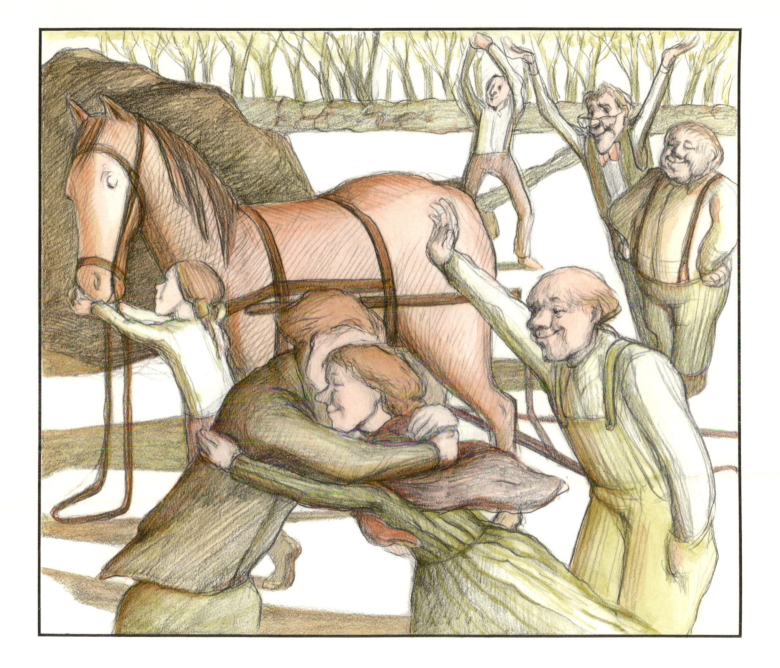

I pulled on Papa's sleeve till he looked down at me. "Well? Well? You got a bee in your bonnet?"

"Did you know about it, Papa?"

Papa roared. " 'Course, I knew how to do it! And I didn't want any son-in-law wasn't clever as me! Moses, now, he's all right. Moses is clever. Moses, you're clever." And Papa hit Moses on the back again.

"Aaaaah!" Moses gulped.

On Wealthy's wedding day, I washed my face and brushed out my braids. I put on a pretty print gown. Even so, I saw in the kitchen dresser mirror that I was not pretty. In fact, I was plain. "Mandy Jane," I said to myself, "you are plain." But I didn't care. "You know," I told myself, "there's few so clever as you, Mandy Jane!"